yPerry
AF443685
JEFF JENKINS AND MIRANDA YOUNG

ACKNOWLEDGEMENTS

Miranda thanks James and Max, Archie, Somer, Wendy, Jeffie J, MW and Jess, Mike B and the greatest writer of all time, Fyodor Dostoevsky.

Jeff thanks Cory & Heidi O'Bryan, Deb Withers, Lucy Mariani, Miranda Young, Pat Delves & Megan Bowe, John Cain, Matty Harem and the Michaels – Wilkinson and Bannenberg.

National Library of Australia Cataloguing-in-Publication entry

Author: Jenkins, Jeff, 1969-

Title: Katy Perry Dream Girl / Jeff Jenkins and Miranda Young.

ISBN: 9781921804359 (pbk.)

Subjects: Perry, Katy, 1984-
             Singers--United States--Biography.

Other Authors/Contributors: Young, Miranda.

Dewey Number: 782.42164092

Photos and illustrations by agreement with international agencies, photographers and illustrators including Rex, Wenn, PA and others.

Design: Michael Bannenberg

Published by:
Wilkinson Publishing Pty Ltd ACN 006 042 173
Level 4, 2 Collins Street Melbourne, Victoria, Australia 3000
Ph: +61 3 9654 5446
www.wilkinsonpublishing.com.au

International distribution by Pineapple Media Limited
(www.pineapple-media.com) ISSN 1838-4447

DreamGirl

When Katheryn Elizabeth Hudson took Katy Perry as her stage name she set in motion a series of events that resulted in her being one of this decade's biggest pop starlets. She deviated from her pre-ordained career path as a Christian singer and began to tear herself a new place in the crowded fabric of international fame as the perfect retro pop star!

Newly wed to the devilishly handsome and deliciously damaged Russell Brand, this dream girl for so many loves the music spotlight and all the lyrical boundaries she can push. Blessed with girl-next-door good looks and a fun '50s burlesque fashion sense that knows no shame, this sweet, sunny Californian, and dearly loved daughter of two pastors, has set a new benchmark for all female pop singers! Katy Perry is a fantastic fusion of fashion eccentricities and serious singing talent; with only two albums behind her she already has major status and major promise in the music business.

There's no doubting the fact there are some basic rules to becoming a Pop Goddess. **THE FIRST RULE OF POP** is *Cuteness*, which makes their *Controversy* so forgivable. Releasing her first internet single in 2007, *Ur So Gay*, Katy started getting some serious left field attention, but it was her second controversial single, *I Kissed A Girl*, in 2008, from the mainstream album *One Of The Boys*, which had her topping the charts in more than 25 countries. The world media readily accepted this soft-core bi-sexual anthem because its "messenger" looked and sang like the girl-next-door. Her second album, *Teenage Dream*, features a painting by Will Cotton, which has Katy lying naked on cotton candy clouds. The Mona Lisa-like smile on Katy's face makes the pose seem as innocent as Renaissance cupids reclining. The first single from this album, *California Gurls*, took only four weeks to reach the number one spot on the Billboard Hot 100, making it the fastest-rising single from a Capitol Records' artist since 1967. The music video, featuring cupcake breast guns spurting whipped cream, is harmless candy pop at its best.

Katy is also aware of what works in the pop world. Just as Alanis Morissette – one of Katy's musical influences – set the world on fire with lyrics about the scorned woman, Katy has embraced the controversial pop song to perfection. Katy also used the same producer, Glen Ballard, for her debut album as Morissette's *Jagged Little Pill* and the same writer and producer, Max Martin, as Britney worked with on … *Baby One More Time*.

Clearly, Katy is not a copy of anyone else – she is distinct and original. A '50s pin-up with swagger and no shame or regrets about anything. Marrying Russell Brand has garnered her front covers of magazines all around the world. Their huge celebrity wedding staged in India has, against the odds, maintained an earthy and romantic feel. Brand said, "I'm trying to preserve and make it a beautiful thing … really, love between two people is the most spectacular and ordinary thing in the world."

Young Katy has even had her appearance on *Sesame Street* with Elmo canned, as her outfit was deemed too racy for pre-schoolers. Katy was actually wearing a flesh-coloured mesh top that went all the way to her neck, but she didn't kick up a fuss and moved on. She has nailed the First Rule of Pop and her style of public and personal controversy is never boring and always fun.

The **SECOND RULE OF POP** is that the artist's work must always be *Cutting Edge*. The latest technology has to be embraced and Katy is all over every branch of music New Media: Twitter, YouTube and social networks throughout the Internet. To date, she has sold more than 22 million digital tracks and mobile products worldwide. Microsoft has signed Katy to bring their search engine BING out of Google's shadow. Following on from her enormously successful Tap Tap Revenge mobile game app for iPhone there is Katy Perry Revenge by Bing – and it's free. Her world tours sell out and she is a constant presence at music award ceremonies and effortlessly charming, yet irreverent on countless TV talk shows, even fronting up as a guest judge on *American Idol*.

The **THIRD RULE OF POP** is *Creativity*. Katy's unconventional fashion sense is bright and unforgiving. She combines a retro '50s feel with some serious candy accessories, with her vintage ingénue style clearly influenced by the fashions of her favorite film, *Lolita*. Not unlike Gwen Stefani, whose own distinct fashion sense and dance is vital to her image, Katy, importantly, is involved in the writing of all her own material and has a cathartic need to express her inner-self through lyrics.

The **FOURTH RULE OF POP** is a healthy does of *Charisma*. Katy is larger than life and unrepentant about it.

"I had a very strong vision and some record companies didn't like that, but I waited for the right one and took a chance. I was lucky because it doesn't always pay off."

You must have this magical fourth element, this magnetic aura that sets you apart from the crowd. With her enviable young vocal range and major guitar skills, Katy Perry's talents always make a lasting impression.

"I always try to make a lasting impression and I work very hard. My father has a saying, 'You can't be a flash in the pan.'"

Pop's new dream girl has a bright future, her new *California Dream* Tour will be more like a Broadway show – stimulating all the fans' senses in a Festival of Perry sights and sounds – like her Cotton Candy scented *Teenage Dream* album cover. Katy, like all the other pop star stayers, has her own fragrance called *Purr*, which comes in a cat-shaped bottle. She is also set to make her film debut, starring in the 2011 film *The Smurfs*, as Smurfette.

Her single *Firework* was inspired by a quote her lover Russell Brand repeated from *American Beat* writer Jack Kerouac's groundbreaking novel *On The Road*:

"The only people for me are the mad ones, the ones who are mad to live, mad to talk, mad to be saved, desirous of everything at the same time, the ones who never yawn or say a commonplace thing, but burn, burn, burn like fabulous yellow roman candles, exploding like spiders across the stars."

This is a mantra to America's new cheeky dream girl whose dream seems to be to have fun, constantly evolve her talent and never submit to musical boundaries.

Dream Weaver

Not since *Footloose* has there been such a remarkable tale of religion and rock.

When Katy Perry was a child, pop music wasn't allowed in her house "because it's the devil's work". She wasn't allowed to eat any sugar. And if Katy brought any friends home, her mum would ask if they were Christians.

But the preacher's daughter grew up to become one of the world's most provocative pop stars.

In one of her first magazine interviews, Katy told *Blender* in 2004: "I'm completely outrageous and I'll do anything for attention." Now – as *Q* magazine states – she has become pop's chief mischief-maker.

So is Katy Perry a good girl gone bad? Or a bad girl who's good? And why has she connected with so many people?

Well, in an era of one-dimensional, predictable pop stars, Katy is full of surprises, declaring, "I'm obsessively, compulsively involved in everything that I do, and I'm always going to take chances.

"And as much as I am that girl who *Kissed A Girl* and that girl who gave the middle-finger to her ex-boyfriend, there's a very different side of me.

"I am a typical woman with many different personalities."

"Did I kiss a girl?
Oh yes, and it was
delightful."

When Katy released the *One Of The Boys* album, she had two simple goals: To do a sold-out tour and meet as many people as possible.

"It's important for me to make a connection with people," Katy explains. "I think people have this perception of pop girls, that they're unreachable, that they're from another planet. But I actually like being from Earth and I like meeting people.

"I give out hugs, not handshakes. I'm not scared of meeting my fans. These people are so wonderful and I'm very appreciative."

Katy still knows what it's like to be a fan. When Madonna invited her backstage after her London show, all Katy could stammer – as Gwyneth Paltrow looked on – was "thank you".

"It was definitely a pee-in-my-pants moment," Katy recalls.

Katy Perry is a rarity in more ways than one — she's a pop star who actually enjoys doing interviews. Even as her interrogators persisted with the one line of inquiry: *Have you really kissed a girl?*, Katy was not fazed. "It's exciting for me to answer any questions," she points out. "It's great that people are interested and by doing interviews, I get to promote my music."

Katy doesn't pretend she's perfect, confessing, "I've got flaws, most definitely." And she doesn't even mind being compared to other artists. "I understand that people want to compare," she says. "I have black hair and big eyes, so I have a Lily Allen factor. Or I'm a pop/rock girl, so people mention Avril Lavigne … Go ahead, I don't find it offensive.

"But," she adds, "I'm trying to carve a path of my own."

Katy actually started the comparisons by writing on her MySpace page that she sounded like "a fatter version of Amy Winehouse and a skinnier Lily Allen". Lily was not amused. And then there's Katy's music. She might not have been allowed any sugar when she was a child, but Katy can come up with a pop hook so sweet it nearly rots your teeth.

"How many times do you turn on the radio and you're like, 'What the hell is this song about?'" Katy asks. "You can feel the beat and I guess you're supposed to dance to it, but you can't sing along.

"I wanna sing along to a song!"

To prepare for the *Teenage Dream* album, Katy made a mixtape of her favourite "fun female songs", including The Cardigans' *Lovefool*, The Bangles' *Manic Monday* and Divinyls' *I Touch Myself*. "That was my reference," Katy reveals. "Not that I was copying, but that was the brightness that I wanted. I was making a great fun pop record."

> "I live this fantastic life, full of all these magical things."

It might be pop, but there is depth. "I always want to tell a story with my songs," Katy adds. "That's my thing – I'm a storyteller. Even though they're fun pop songs, there's always a story behind them."

One song on the *One Of The Boys* album was called *Waking Up In Vegas*. Katy laughs when she recounts her own "Vegas moment". "My dad and I are both practical jokers," she smiles, "so when I was 21, I went to Vegas with my boyfriend at the time. We bought a wedding dress and a tux and we went to a little white chapel and got 'fake married.'" Katy sent the photos and the fake marriage certificate to her mum and dad. "They freaked out, while we were laughing like devils. My dad then thought it was a good joke."

The other part of the Katy Perry package is the look – from her "fruity" outfits to her striking blue hair, Katy is always going to be noticed.

Before she was a star, Katy recalls having a night on the town with a friend. Katy was wearing a big red velvet 1940s coat. Her friend looked at her and smiled. "You know what, Katy, if you ever make it, they're gonna say something about the way you dress."

She was right.

When Katy hit the charts, she started getting almost as much attention for her often outrageous outfits. "I'm a sucker for a theme," she laughs. Her fashion polarises people – she often appears on both best and worst dressed lists. But Katy doesn't mind. "Everyone has an opinion. I just dress for myself and it makes me happy. And it makes other people smile. I guess I'm just a big personality. I've always been this way."

Katy admires the dress sense of Pixie Geldof, Peaches, Kelly Osbourne and supermodel Agyness Deyn. "Girls who just have their own sense of style, I just love that.

"It's fun being a girl," she adds, "and you just can't explain that to the boys."

Katy Perry wanted to be a musician ever since she started playing guitar when she was 13. That was a big year for Katy, who was beginning to assert her independence. When her mum refused to let her get a piercing, Katy went ahead and pierced her own nose – with a safety pin. "Don't try this at home," she laughs, "even though it actually didn't look too bad."

Katy's mum and dad wanted her to make Christian music, but Katy – inspired by Gwen Stefani, Shirley Manson and Alanis Morissette – secretly longed to be a pop star. And her idol was Queen's Freddie Mercury. "He was very theatrical and

"My personality is up and down, sassy and cheeky."

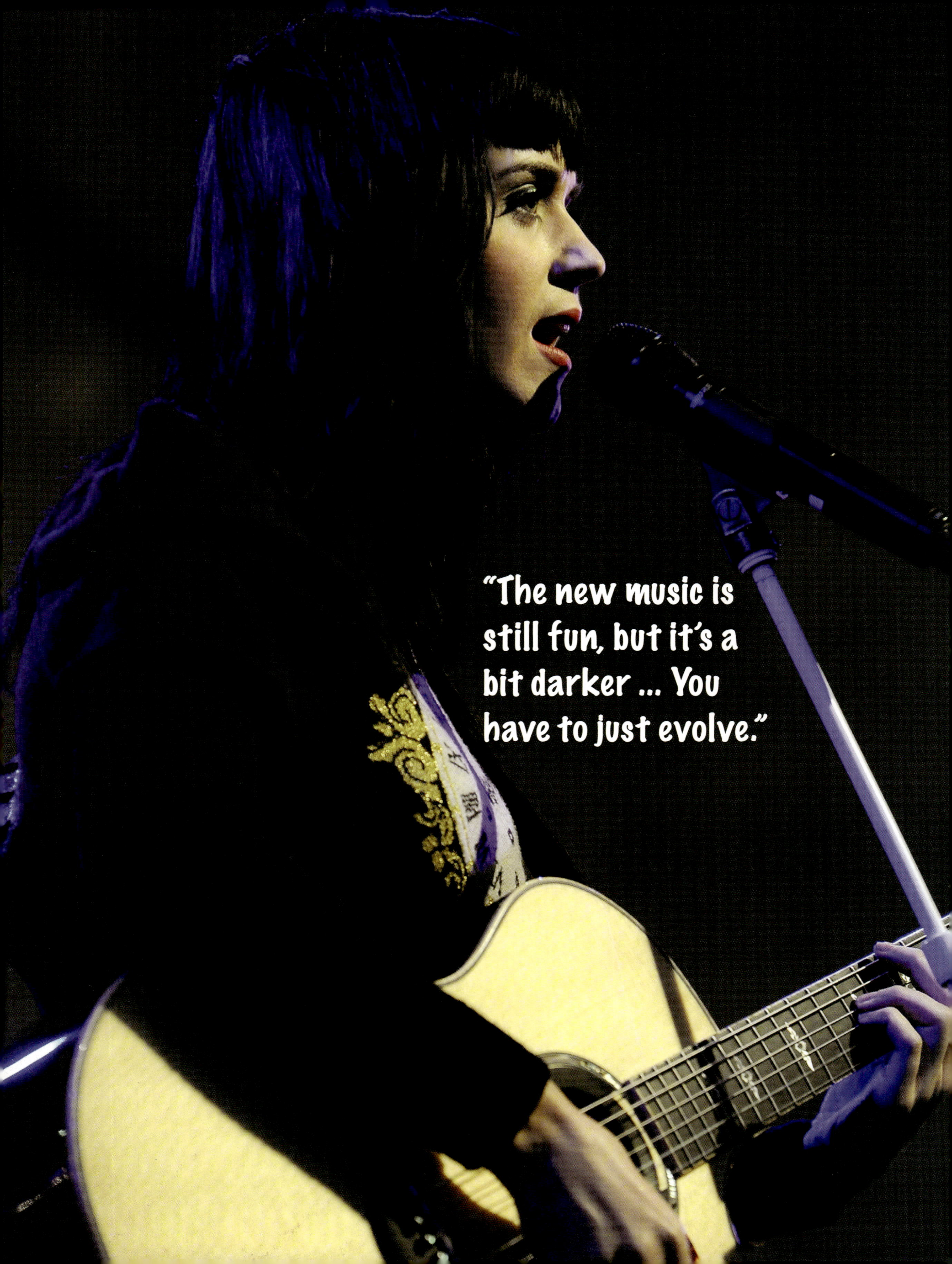
"The new music is still fun, but it's a bit darker ... You have to just evolve."

"I have always been this character, but I kind of cartoon-ised myself a little bit."

flamboyant and he always said what he wanted and didn't care what anyone thought."

Two days before her 17th birthday, Katy released her debut album – a self-titled gospel pop collection (released under Katy's birth name – *Katy Hudson*). Asked what she sounded like back then, Katy replies: "I was Christian but modern." The album featured songs called *Trust In Me* and *Faith Won't Fail*. It was not a hit, and Katy's label went out of business.

Fast forward a few years – and a few false starts – Katy Perry was such a star, even her cat was nominated for an award. "She's got a story of her own," Katy smiles. "If only she could say more than meow."

The stray cat came into Katy's life when she bounded through the window of the home of Katy's then boyfriend. Katy was not impressed. "I hated cats, I was such a dog person." Katy's boyfriend called the cat Rat Montgomery III, but didn't want to keep her when he and Katy broke up. "By this stage, I'd fallen in love with her, but I had to change her name. I said, 'From now on, her name will be Kitty Purry and she will have a wonderful life.'"

Katy loves that cats are independent but dependable. "I know I will be the crazy cat lady and that when I'm 50 I will have 50 cats, but I'm okay with that." Katy's fans are even called "Katy Cats".

As for Kitty Purry, she was up for an award at the 2009 Teen Choice Awards. But she was beaten by President Obama's dog, Bo, who took the trophy for Choice Celebrity Pet.

Appropriately, the title track of Katy's breakthrough album was a coming-of-age tale. "*One Of The Boys* is a song that talks about that moment where you go from junior high to high school," Katy explains, "and you turn from an ugly ducking into a swan. Guys no longer want to make fun of you, they want to make out with you."

Katy's favourite song on the *One Of The Boys* album is *Thinking of You*. "I'm very proud of it," she says. "I wrote it by myself in my little apartment and it's very sincere. It's a song about regret and loss and struggling to get over that last person."

Katy admits she's a sucker for love. "When I fall in love, I fall really hard. It's always deep – let's-get-married deep. When I was 16 and going through a break-up, it was the end of the world. I was very depressed and freaking out. But I was told that there are many fish in the sea. And that's very true – there are many fish in the sea. And I believe there's the right shape out there for everybody."

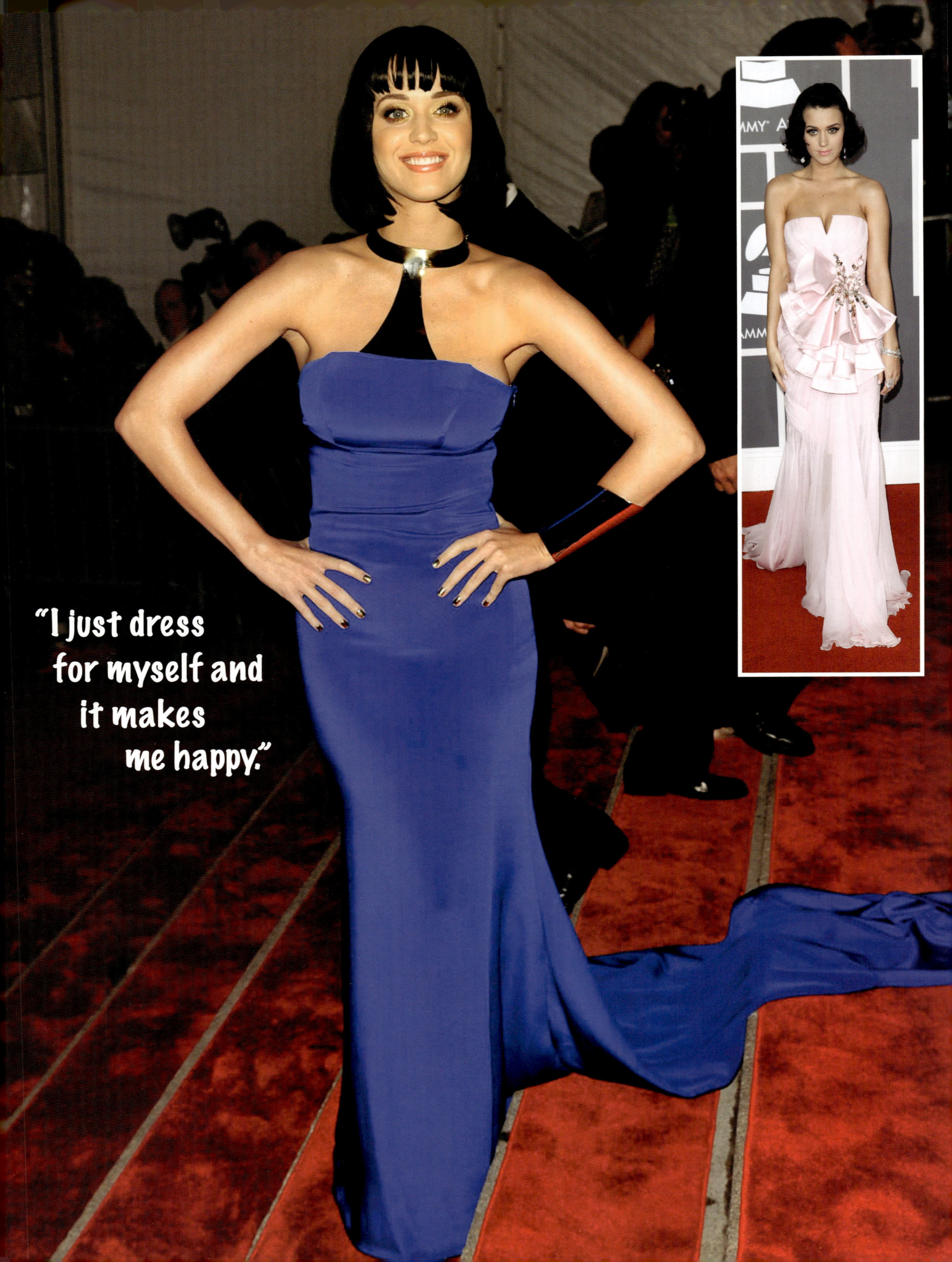

"I just dress
for myself and
it makes
me happy."

No wonder she ended up with one of the world's hottest comedians. Even before she'd met Russell Brand, Katy revealed: "I'm really attracted to funny boys. I don't care if they're covered in zits or if they don't have hair, if they can make me laugh, they take the cake."

But is Katy a high-maintenance girl? "No, I'm not," she asserts, "I just know exactly what I want."

Another real-life relationship inspired one of Katy's biggest hits, *Hot n Cold*. "That's a song about those boys who don't know what they want. I remember being with a guy and he was like, 'Let's go out to dinner tonight.' I was like, cool, it's a date, and I went home and spent four hours getting ready. Then he called and said, 'I'm just gonna hang with the boys tonight.'" Katy has a term for not knowing what you want in a relationship: "*Love bipolar*".

It was widely reported that Katy's parents were aghast when she became a pop star, angry that she was promoting homosexuality with *I Kissed A Girl*. But Mr and Mrs Perry are actually very proud of their daughter. "My parents are fantastic and I love them so much and they love me too, even though I might not have turned out exactly as they'd hoped."

But Katy has not turned her back on her faith. She still considers herself a Christian, stating, "God is very much still a part of my life."

If there's one Biblical story that Katy can relate to it's the *Book of Job*, the tale of the God-fearing man who loses his health and his wealth, but never gives up or loses his faith. And the patience of Job is rewarded by riches he could never have imagined.

It took Katy five years and three record companies before she became a star. "It was like having it all and losing it all, and then having it all and losing it all," she says of her run of failed recording deals.

Some of the pain of rejection lingers, but Katy Perry is now happy, knowing that all her detractors and critics have been proven wrong.

"I really feel that I have it all now."

Success is sweet for Katy because it didn't come easily. Her sister often reminds her of the times when she was flat broke, selling her clothes just so she could eat.

Not many artists survive being dropped by their record company. "A lot of people said I was damaged goods," Katy acknowledges, "or that I was no good. But I guess I'm living proof that if you hang in there and believe in yourself and don't give up, then you can survive any setbacks."

Yep, dreams can come true.

"Ultimately, I want Katy Perry to be as much of a household name as Madonna."

"Any artist who says they
don't Google their name
is a big fat liar."

"I can't run from where I came from,
nobody can."

THE KATY TIMELINE

October 25, 1984: Katheryn Elizabeth Hudson is born in Santa Barbara, California.

1999: Katy signs to the Christian music label Red Hill.

October 2001: Katy releases her debut album, a self-titled set of gospel pop songs (under the name *Katy Hudson*).

2003: Katy signs to the Island Def Jam label and makes an album that is not released.

2004: Katy is dropped by the Def Jam label and signs to Columbia. She makes another album that is not released.

October 2004: Katy is declared "The Next Big Thing" by *Blender* magazine. Katy tells the magazine she is obsessed with "Paris, France, Kate Moss, and lint rollers – they clean anything!"

May 2005: Katy has a song, *Simple*, on the soundtrack to the movie *The Sisterhood Of The Traveling Pants*.

2006: Katy is dropped by Columbia Records.

January 2006: Katy sings on the P.O.D single *Goodbye For Now* and appears in the video.

November 2006: Katy appears in the video for Gym Class Heroes' *Cupid's Chokehold*, playing the love interest of her boyfriend, Travis McCoy.

2007: Katy signs with Capitol Music and adopts the stage name "Katy Perry".

November 2007: Katy releases her first internet single, *Ur So Gay*.

March 2008: Katy appears as herself in the US TV series *Wildfire*, in an episode called "Life's Too Short".

May 2008: *I Kissed A Girl* is released.

June 2008: Katy hits the road as part of the Warped Tour. She appears as herself in the soap opera *The Young And The Restless*. The first Katy Perry album, *One Of The Boys*, is released.

July 2008: *I Kissed A Girl* knocks off Coldplay's *Viva La Vida* to hit number one in the US (July 5). Katy celebrates with a bottle of Dom Perignon in Vegas. The single spends seven weeks on top. It also spends six weeks at number one in Australia.

August 2008: *I Kissed A Girl* hits number one in the UK, spending five weeks on top.

September 2008: *Hot n Cold* is released. It hits number three in the US, and four in Australia and the UK.

November 2008: Katy hosts the MTV Europe Music Awards and takes the trophy for Best New Act.

December 2008: Katy breaks up with Travis McCoy.

January 2009: Katy's first headlining tour, the Hello Katy Tour, starts in Seattle. *Thinking of You* is released as a single. It peaks at 27 in the UK, 29 in the US, and 34 in Australia. A fan pays $3500 for a plaster cast mold of Katy's breasts. "That's a lot of money in a recession," Katy says.

February 2009: *I Kissed A Girl* is up for Best Female Pop Vocal Performance at the Grammy Awards. The Grammy goes to Adele's *Chasing Pavements*. Katy wins Best International Female Artist at the BRIT Awards.

March 2009: Katy wins Best Breakthrough Artist at the MTV Australia Awards.
Kelly Clarkson releases her fourth album, *All I Ever Wanted*, featuring a song co-written by Katy, *I Do Not Hook Up*. It becomes the album's second single, hitting number nine in Australia. "I was beyond flattered that Kelly Clarkson would do one of my songs," Katy says.

April 2009: *Waking Up In Vegas* is released as a single. It peaks at number nine in the US, 11 in Australia, and 19 in the UK.

June 2009: Lesbian pop star Beth Ditto slams Katy, telling *Attitude* magazine: "I hate Katy Perry! She's offensive to gay culture, I'm so offended. She's just riding on the backs of our culture." Katy replied: "I've learned in the past year that one artist should never insult another artist's music – it's tacky."

July 2009: Katy does an *MTV Unplugged* gig in New York. Katy films a cameo for the Russell Brand movie *Get Him To The Greek*, but the scene doesn't make the final cut. She later jokes to Russell: "I was, like, sleeping with you and you're not gonna put me in the movie? That's so messed up!"

September 2009: Katy appears on a remix of the 3OH!3 single *Starstrukk*. The song hits the Top 5 in Australia and the UK. Katy starts dating Russell Brand.

October 2009: Katy starts recording the *Teenage Dream* album.

November 2009: Katy's *MTV Unplugged* album is released, featuring six of her own songs and a cover of Fountain of Wayne's *Hackensack*.

December 2009: Katy and Russell Brand get engaged. Katy appears on the Timbaland single *If We Ever Meet Again*. It hits the Top 10 in Australia and the UK. *Billboard* declares Katy one of the Top 100 Artists Of The Decade.

February 2010: *Hot n Cold* is up for Best Female Pop Vocal Performance at the Grammy Awards. The Grammy goes to Beyonce's *Halo*.

March 2010: It's announced that Katy will make her movie debut providing the voice of Smurfette in *The Smurfs* movie – even though she was not allowed to watch *The Smurfs* when she was a child. "My parents felt that the Smurfs' reliance on sorcery and magic sent the wrong messages to children."

May 2010: Katy releases *California Gurls*, featuring Snoop Dogg, the first single from the *Teenage Dream* album. It hits number one in the US (June 19), spending six weeks on top.

June 2010: *California Gurls* hits number one in Australia (June 21). It spends four weeks on top.

July 2010: *California Gurls* debuts at number one in the UK (July 3), spending two weeks on top.

August 2010: The second Katy Perry album, *Teenage Dream*, is released. The CD booklet smells like cotton candy. "CDs are over," Katy says, "but not if they smell original." The album debuts at number one in the US, Australia and UK.

September 2010: Katy opens the new season of *Saturday Night Live*. The *Teenage Dream* single hits number one in the US, spending two weeks on top. Katy sings *Hot n Cold* with Elmo for the season premiere of *Sesame Street*, but the producers decide that it's too hot for the show and it ends up being shown only online.

October 2010: Katy releases *Firework*, the third single from the *Teenage Dream* album. Katy and Russell Brand get married in India (October 23).

November 2010: Katy launches her own perfume called "Purr".

December 2010: Katy plays Moe's girlfriend in an episode of *The Simpsons*, "The Fight Before Christmas".

February 2011: The California Dreams Tour kicks off in Lisbon, Portugal (February 20).

"I am a typical woman
with many
different personalities."

Son (and daughter) of a preacher man

Katy Perry is not the only pop star with preachers for parents.

ARETHA FRANKLIN
The Queen of Soul started singing in church. Her dad was a famous Baptist minister, Reverend C. L. Franklin, who even recorded and released some of his famous sermons.

ALICE COOPER
The father of shock rocker Alice Cooper (real name: Vincent Furnier) was a lay preacher in The Church of Jesus Christ, while his grandfather was a Church apostle.

TORI AMOS
Tori Amos, who led the wave of female singer-songwriters in the '90s, is the daughter of a Methodist minister. In 2009, she released an album called *Abnormally Attracted To Sin*.

CASSIE DAVIS
This Perth singer – whose debut single, *Like It Loud*, hit number 11 in Australia – grew up singing in the church where her dad, Steven, was a pastor. She says, "I never want to make my father disappointed or ashamed that I'm his daughter." Cassie even did a single, *Differently*, featuring Katy's ex Travis McCoy.

JIMMY WEBB
Jimmy's dad, Robert Lee Webb, was a Baptist minister who would only let his son listen to country and gospel music. Jimmy ended up writing such classics as *Wichita Lineman, Galveston, By The Time I Get To Phoenix* and *MacArthur Park.*

MARVIN GAYE
Marvin Gaye – famous for the hits *I Heard It Through The Grapevine* and *Sexual Healing* – was the son of Marvin Sr, a minister at the House of God. But the Prince of Soul was shot dead by his dad on April 1, 1984.

LEMMY
Motorhead are in the *Guinness Book of Records* as the loudest band ever. The father of lead singer Lemmy (full name: Ian Fraser Kilmister) was a chaplain in the Royal Air Force. But his parents broke up when he was a baby and Lemmy was 25 before he saw his dad again.

KINGS OF LEON
The three Followill brothers – Caleb, Nathan and Jared – grew up travelling across the US. Their dad, Leon, was a travelling preacher with the United Pentecostal Church. But he left the church because he had a drinking problem.

THE STUDIO ALBUMS

Katy Hudson
(did not chart, 2001)
Trust In Me/ Piercing/ Search Me/ Last Call/ Growing Pains/ My Own Monster/ Split/ Faith Won't Fail/ Naturally/ When There's Nothing Left

"A gifted songwriter in her own right who will almost certainly go far in this business."
Christianity Today

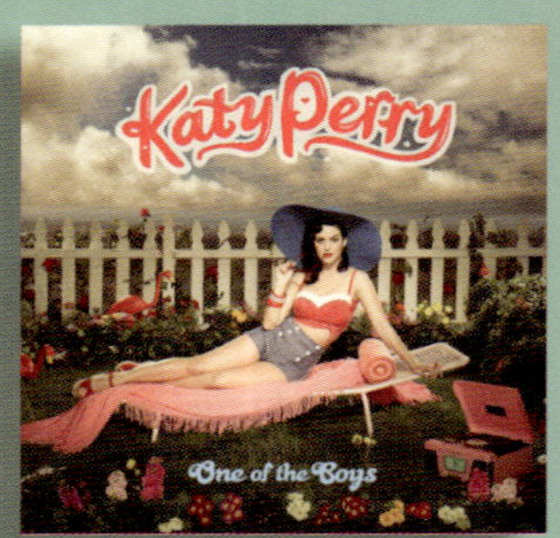

One Of The Boys
(#9 US, 11 in Australia and UK, 2008)
One Of The Boys/ I Kissed A Girl/ Waking Up In Vegas/ Thinking of You/ Mannequin/ Ur So Gay/ Hot n Cold/ If You Can Afford Me/ Lost/ Self Inflicted/ I'm Still Breathing/ Fingerprints

"Not since *Jagged Little Pill* has a debut album been so packed with potential hits." – *Billboard*

MTV Unplugged (#168 US, 2009)
I Kissed A Girl/ Ur So Gay/ Hackensack/ Thinking of You/ Lost/ Waking Up In Vegas/ Brick By Brick

"She uses the show as a way to re-brand herself as a serious pop auteur." – *Allmusic.com*

I'm so excited for my album release on tuesday I might have a Teenage WET Dream tonight. #8.24.10
2:44 PM Aug 23rd via ÜberTwitter

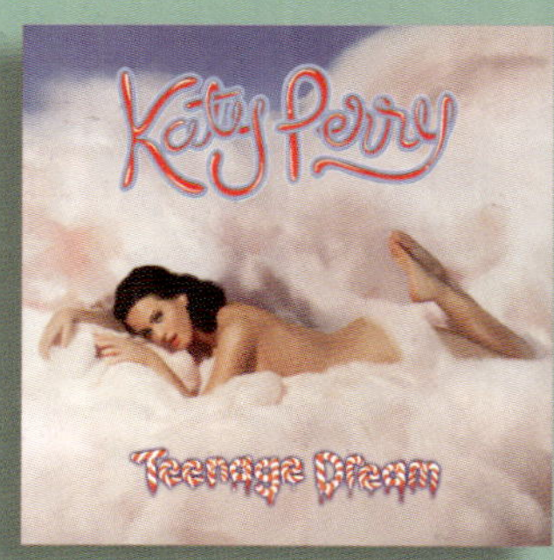

Teenage Dream
(#1 US, Australia & UK, 2010)
Teenage Dream/ Last Friday Night (T.G.I.F)/ California Gurls/ Firework/ Peacock/ Circle The Drain/ The One That Got Away/ E.T/ Who Am I Living For?/ Pearl/ Hummingbird Heartbeat/ Not Like The Movies

"Beneath the fruity outfits and fart jokes, Perry is clearly serious about the business of hit songcraft." – *Entertainment Weekly*

GREAT morning friends! Today is the day I release my NEW album #TEENAGEDREAM! So excited about it, I hope u ♥ it. I hope it makes u smile. *3:42 AM Aug 25th via ÜberTwitter*

"The new music
is still fun, but
it's a bit darker.
It's not as annoying.
You have to just
evolve."

FACTS AND FAVOURITES

Favourite part of the day: Snuggle time with her cat, Kitty Purry

Breakfast: A hard-boiled egg every morning

Zoo animal: A leopard

Domestic animal: Kittens

Colours: Blue, green, brown, yellow, and neon colours

Place to visit: Japan

Foods: Thai, Mexican, French crepes, spaghetti, ice cream

Car: A hybrid

Three "rock star" moments: Eating dinner with Mick Jagger, having a release party for her album, and seeing a full-body tattoo of herself on a fan's arm

Activities: Surfing, weekend trips, garage sales, anything Japanese, theme dressing, rollerblading, ice-skating, miniature golf

Movies: *Romeo + Juliet* (1996), *Lolita* (both 1962 and 1997), *Blade Runner* (1982), *The Professional* (1994), *The Notebook* (2004)

TV shows: *The Office* ("the American version"), *The Real Housewives of New Jersey, Flight Of The Conchords, Saved By The Bell*, any documentaries about child beauty pageants

Books: *All You Need to Know About the Music Business, Me Talk Pretty One Day, Are You There God? It's Me, Margaret, The Help,The Book of Proverbs*

Musicians: Queen, The Beach Boys, Madonna, Patty Griffin, Paul Simon

Inspirational people: Jesus, Gandhi, Freddie Mercury, Paul Newman, Angelina Jolie

KATY FACTS

- Katy's real last name is Hudson. But she uses her mum's surname because she doesn't want to be confused with actress Kate Hudson.

- Katy's natural hair colour is dirty blond.

- Katy called her cat Kitty Purry. Russell's cat is called Morrissey. They also have a kitten called Krusty.

- Katy's dad has four tattoos – all of which say JESUS.

- *Cobra Starship* covered Katy's biggest hit as *I Kissed A Boy*. Robert Lund did it as *I Peed In The Pool*. Katy calls these covers "Katy Perodies". Her favourite is *I Kissed A Nerd*.

"I really feel that I have it all now."